STUART,
A HANDY THING
TO KEEP BY
YOUR BED, TO

SEE WHAT
TOMORROW
MIGHT BRING!
LOVE
FIONA x

ROMANY GYPSY HOROSCOPES

JAMES PETULENGRO

PISCES

MILLENNIUM HOROSCOPES

2000

BROCKHAMPTON PRESS

With thanks to:
Darren Hanson, Karen Hanson, Alvin Hanson, Simon and Laurner,
Paul and Elspeth, Mark Anguluccy, Ian Sanderson, Eve, Kay, Shane,
Eric and Honer Boswell

With special thanks to my mum Leonora Petulengro and
my special friend Paula Paradema.

First published in the United Kingdom in 1999
by Brockhampton Press Limited
20 Bloomsbury Street
London WC1B 3QA
a member of the Hodder Headline PLC Group

© 1998 Brockhampton Press Limited

Designed and produced for Brockhampton Press by
Open Door Limited,
80 High Street, Colsterworth,
Lincolnshire NG33 5JA

Editing: Penny Sucharov
Design and illustration: Open Door Limited
Colour separation: GA Graphics, Stamford, UK

Printed at Oriental Press, Dubai, U.A.E.

Title: PISCES
ISBN: 1-86019-911-9

PISCES
2000

♓

CONTENTS

ROMANY PROFILE OF PISCES

Symbol:	*The fishes*
Ruling planet:	*Neptune*
Best traits:	*Compassion, imagination and intuition*
Worst traits:	*Indecision, irrationality and easily influenced*
Colours:	*Turquoise and sea-green*
Birthstone:	*Aquamarine and turquoise*
Metal:	*Pewter*
Element:	*Water*
Season:	*Winter*
Lucky numbers:	*3 and 12*
Best day:	*Thursday*
Worst day:	*Wednesday*

♓

Pisces is the twelfth sign of the zodiac and governs the feet and veins. It is symbolised by two fish pointing in opposite directions and is one of the three water signs. Pisces is also symbolised by the season of winter and its influence lasts from 19th February to 20th March.

Pisces is ruled by the planet Jupiter, the planet of money and wisdom, and Neptune, the planet of dreams and visions. This is probably why Pisceans are known as the dreamers of the zodiac. They are definitely not the most practical of people and when it comes to hands-on work they can have great difficulty. However, if you want creative concepts then they are the people to ask and they will probably come up with an idea that you would never have dreamed of.

To others, Pisceans often come across as a little distant or even a little slow, but this is just because their mind is usually elsewhere in their own daydreams. They are also quite indecisive and as such can often be swayed by others who may be more direct or forceful. Sensitive to a fault, the Piscean can be greatly upset by thoughtless or cruel remarks and other people should be warned to choose their words carefully.

The Piscean friend is one of the best friends a person could ask for. They are sensitive and caring and always make time to listen to others' problems. However, their friends should also prepare themselves to listen to the Piscean's problems which will usually be some sort of worry over something which may or may not happen. If you want someone to stand by you in a crisis, the Piscean is the friend you need.

Emotionally Pisceans are extremely sensitive, if not over-sensitive. They are ruled by their emotions and are usually

in need of reassurance from the people around them. If they don't get this support they can be prone to very negative thoughts and feelings, even severe depression.

In love, the Piscean can very often be disappointed as their prospective partners rarely live up to the romantic ideal that they have in their head. The perfect partner for a Piscean is someone who is also a friend, and many long-term partners for Pisces people will start out as just that. The main thing a Piscean looks for from a partner is emotional support, as they need someone to tell their worries to who will tell them everything will be all right. They also need a certain amount of freedom in a relationship as feeling trapped can make them very unhappy.

The Piscean loves to be a parent and will shower their children with affection. They want their children to have the best in life and can sometimes be accused of spoiling their offspring by catering to their every want. The problems start, however, when the child wants some independence, as the Piscean parent will worry constantly and want to wrap the child in cotton wool, which can cause arguments and hurt feelings.

Healthwise, the Piscean is not the best patient – they are usually better at caring for others than for themselves. They should be especially careful of problems with their feet as Pisces is linked to this area of the body. The Piscean's emotional feelings can also greatly affect their health both negatively and positively.

The Piscean's home will usually be a calming homely place where the Piscean can feel safe and secure. They generally avoid loud or bright colours and usually prefer soothing and

pale colours. They have a knack for mixing and matching and often buy things from several places which will go together as if they were especially designed to. Pisceans are not generally great lovers of organised hobbies, much preferring to go their own way, doing things that they enjoy. They usually love to just wander around their garden or the surrounding countryside without any particular goal in mind, doing whatever takes their fancy at that moment. Arts and crafts of various types are also popular with Pisceans, but only when they are in the right mood.

On the career front, Pisceans love a job where they can use their imagination and like to put forward their ideas in the workplace. As they are very creative people, jobs involving writing or designing attract them, as do jobs which involve problem-solving. They also love to help with people and are often drawn to the caring professions where they feel that they are making a difference. They also make good vets, teachers and artists.

FAMOUS PISCEANS

Michael Caine, Albert Einstein, Prince Edward, Fréderic Chopin, George Handel, Elizabeth Taylor, Michelangelo, Prince Andrew, Mikhail Gorbachev, Rudolf Nureyev, Enrico Caruso and Alexander Graham Bell.

COMPATIBILITY WITH PISCES

Pisces and Pisces

There will be a definite attraction between these two as they will instantly understand each other. However this is just the problem. These two will know exactly how to hurt each other, so that arguments will be hurtful and personal. They have very little chance of staying together for long.

Score 3/10. Too similar to really work.

Pisces and Aries

Equality is the buzz-word for this pairing. As long as these signs respect each other's differences this can be a good match. Ariens and Pisceans can learn a lot from each other and this match can turn into a relationship of constantly expanding horizons where the sky is the limit.

Score 8/10. Good going with a little work.

Pisces and Taurus

This match will be difficult from the start as the Piscean and Taurean have almost nothing in common. The sympathetic, dreamy fish is almost certain to be trodden on by the straightforward bull, and the Piscean moods are bound to get on the Taurean's nerves.

Score 2/10. A poor pairing.

Pisces and Gemini

Practicality is neither of these individuals' strong point and because of this their relationship will suffer. Both are too busy daydreaming or having fun to concentrate on making their relationship stronger. They will need outside help if this partnership is to work.

Score 3/10. Not a good match.

Pisces and Cancer

Emotions rule in this match. Cancerians and Pisceans are quite good at seeing each other's points of view. If the Piscean can give the Cancerian the support they need and the Cancerian can let the Piscean have solitude when it is needed, this match can work well.

Score 8/10. Good, with a little give and take.

Pisces and Leo

This relationship will tend to be quite one-sided as the Piscean will usually be more committed to making things work than the Leo. Leo will take advantage of this to have his own way and will rarely put in any effort. The constant disinterest of the Leo will usually make even the most stubborn Pisces think twice about staying in this relationship.

Score 2/10. Not a good match.

Pisces and Virgo

Although these two have very little in common, this can in fact work in their favour. Both are willing to give the other enough space to be themselves, which will tend to avoid arguments. Both are different enough from the other that their interests and priorities will very rarely clash.

Score 6/10. A fairly good match.

Pisces and Libra

It is generally unlikely that these two will ever get a relationship off the ground as they have almost nothing in common. However, if they do, because of their very different natures, each can bring out a side in the other that they may not even have realised they had.

Score 6/10. A good match if it ever gets going.

Pisces and Scorpio

These two have a fairly good chance of lasting as the fussy Piscean will find the moody Scorpio a challenge. The Scorpio in turn will find the understanding they need in the emotional Pisces. Each will keep the other under just enough control so as to keep things interesting.

Score 8/10. An interesting match.

Pisces and Sagittarius

These two will hit problems almost straight away as each has a completely different idea of what a relationship should be like. They will generally take it out on the other when each does not measure up to their ideal. Basically they are just too different.

Score 1/10. A disappointing match for each of them.

Pisces and Capricorn

This relationship has as much chance of not working out as it does of being a big romance. They will definitely be attracted to each other, and if they can agree to disagree on some areas and live with it, they can build a good relationship. However, it can just as easily go the other way and a lot of care is needed on both sides to make things work.

Score 6/10. A real gamble, but can be worth it.

Pisces and Aquarius

This relationship is most definitely one of interesting possibilities. Each can learn a great deal from the other, but neither will want to admit it. Both will fool themselves into thinking they are in control of the other, when really the other is just letting them think this is the case.

Score 6/10. A very complex relationship.

DAY-BY-DAY
HOROSCOPES

2000

♓

JANUARY

January 1st, Saturday

Happy New Year! This coming year will bring many changes for the better to your life and it will certainly be a year to remember. An invitation for a night on the town may come your way. Try to accept this as you will have fun. A very good time lies ahead.

January 2nd, Sunday

Planetary influences indicate that changes for the better are on their way. A new door is about to open and a better direction will be taken. Any problems that you have recently encountered will be resolved.

January 3rd, Monday

Try not to force your opinion on others today, as this situation will need a different approach. Use a tactic that you have tried in the past and this will cast a different light on the matter.

January 4th, Tuesday

This will prove to be a very exciting day, as today will bring a new challenge to your life. You may need to pay a little attention to your finances before they get out of hand. Any problems that you discover now will be sorted out and this will be of benefit in the near future.

January 5th, Wednesday

If you have had the past on your mind, this may give you some inspiration for the future. You will not make the same mistake twice. You may be thinking too deeply. Don't be wooed into a situation that will not benefit you, as you may be wasting your time. A change of direction is needed. Act

today and make a start with something that you have
planned. You will not regret it.

January 6th, Thursday

A family member may need your full attention. Any mishaps
that have occurred in your family will right themselves
today. You will receive some good news and news of travel
will come your way. A stranger who you see in the street will
give you insight into your future; you just may bump into
this person another time.

January 7th, Friday

Look deep into your heart and you will find the solution that
you need to get you through the day. Don't listen to small
talk and certainly don't take seriously any promises that are
made today, as they may be broken. If you need to get things
done, I suggest that you do them yourself today, then you
cannot go wrong and you will not suffer any setbacks

January 8th, Saturday

News of money may come your way today. Don't spend it
before you receive it, as it may take some time before it
reaches your bank account. Lucky numbers which will help
you are 5, 8 and 20 and your age will bring you luck and
play a big part in your life very soon. This is the perfect day
to ask someone for a favour that you have wanted for some
time now. Improvements will come from this which will
make your life a little more bearable.

January 9th, Sunday

Take friends at face value today and don't expect too much
from them as you may feel a little disappointed. Try to go it
alone today as you will get more done. Take care not to take
things out on your loved ones.

January 10th, Monday

A letter that you receive today will give you peace of mind. Try not to worry too much over a family matter as you may be worrying about something that may never happen. News of travel will come to your attention. Plans that you make now will save you time in the near future.

January 11th, Tuesday

Spend time with friends and family as this will be a day to remember. You may receive an invitation to a small party. This should be considered with care before you accept the offer. You just may meet someone whom you have not seen for some time. This may add a little spark to your life, but try not to get too close to the flame as you may get your fingers burned.

January 12th, Wednesday

You may be feeling in a good mood and on top of the world. Don't let anyone spoil your mood or bring you down. Happy times lay just ahead and your love life will give you a big surprise. You are definitely in for a treat. Your personal life is about to take a turn for the better. However, you may need to sort out your finances as you may have neglected this aspect of your life.

January 13th, Thursday

News of a birth may come from a friend. This will surprise not just you, but it will be a surprise to many others. However, this news will make someone very happy. Travel will result from this and someone whom you know will move house. You will be planning a journey soon, but don't be surprised if there is a slight delay.

January 14th, Friday

A friend may come to you with a big problem. You can give them a helping hand as they need your support at the

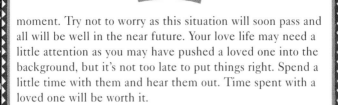

moment. Try not to worry as this situation will soon pass and all will be well in the near future. Your love life may need a little attention as you may have pushed a loved one into the background, but it's not too late to put things right. Spend a little time with them and hear them out. Time spent with a loved one will be worth it.

January 15th, Saturday

You may be falling behind with a business project but you will cover some ground today. You will be in a mood where you will really get things done and your work will not go unnoticed. People that surround you may be telling you their worries and troubles but don't take it to heart, as they probably are just having a good grumble as you are an easy person to talk to. There is news of a forthcomng birth and a family member may be planning a move.

January 16th, Sunday

You may find yourself thinking hard about events which took place in the past. This will ensure that you do not make the same mistake twice. You must forget the hurt that the past has caused as this is all behind you and better times lie directly ahead. Take a good look around you and you'll realise that things are not as bad as they may seem. You may be feeling a little negative. It's time to recharge your batteries and go forward with an open mind.

January 17th, Monday

You may be faced with a major decision today and find yourself confronted with a rather uncompromising situation. Keep calm and all will be well; something that you have lost out on in the past will come back into your life. However, this time it will be more worth-while. Try not to be impatient with a loved one as they may be feeling a little neglected. Pay them some attention and there will be no problems.

January 18th, Tuesday

You may find yourself in unfamiliar surroundings today. A walk in the country or a meal in a country pub with a loved one may be on the agenda. It will give you some inspiration and make your life worthwhile if you make the effort today. Listen to a loved one as they surprise you by what they are about to say. This will open many doors and pave the way for your future.

January 19th, Wednesday

A stranger who wears blue will make themselves known to you today and put a very good opportunity your way. Try to delay accepting this as it may not be the right time to embark on any new business ventures. Put this on hold for a later date and you will reap the rewards in more ways than one.

January 20th, Thursday

Temptation may stand in your way today. Look before you leap, as this situation may be a lot of fun but it may complicate your life and add to your stress. You can do without any extra problems at the moment and you may just get caught in the act and do more harm than good to a relationship. You must get yourself out of this situation at all costs as there will be a better opportunity at a later date.

January 21st, Friday

Don't take the events of today too seriously and let others do the hard work. The day should go smoothly, but if it does not don't panic as it will not be as bad as it appears. A phone call that you receive at work will put you in a good mood as what you hear will really please you.

January 22nd, Saturday

Take time out to have a little fun. Try going somewhere that you have never been before. A shopping spree may be the

answer. You may have had your eye on that certain
something for some time now. This is the right time to treat
yourself. You deserve it. Money matters will improve and a
better position within a work situation is foreseen.

January 23rd, Sunday

Someone who you rely on may let you down, so try not to
depend on them too much. On the whole this will be a
rewarding day. Someone from the past will get in touch
soon, so try to put some time to one side for old times' sake.
It will be worth your while.

January 24th, Monday

Listen to what a friend has to say as this will certainly open
your eyes and cast a different light on a problem that you
have had. A problem shared is a problem halved, and this
will help you to resolve certain things that you have had on
your mind.

January 25th, Tuesday

You may have to use strong words today if you want results. A
tall stranger will bring you luck and the colour red will bring
you money. Changes that happen around you today will be for
the best in the long run, so don't panic if certain matters
change. Love matters are set to improve and someone who
you see through a window may just be your destiny.

January 26th, Wednesday

Planetary influences indicate that you are at a turning point
in your life and things in general will start to run a little
more smoothly. Love is set to improve and those who are
not attached will soon be singing love's song as they have
luck on their side and will attract a partner.

January 27th, Thursday

You will have a strange meeting with someone whom you find very attractive, but you must resist temptation at all cost as you may find yourself in a very awkward situation and you may do damage to an existing relationship.

January 28th, Friday

Someone whom you hold close to your heart may need some advice and you may need to find a little time for them. You may have to return a favour and this may mean that you have to put yourself out for a little while. However, you will be rewarded in the near future and you never know when you just might need a favour in return.

January 29th, Saturday

This week will bring many challenges, but try not to be deterred. With some determination you will battle through. You will overcome any obstacles that you encounter and this will bring you more than you could ever imagine. If you have something on your mind, share it with a friend before you take action. They may help you to see a problem in a different light.

January 30th, Sunday

Another Sunday, but this one will certainly be different as there is a surprise lurking just around the corner which will delight you. Time shared with a loved one will not be wasted as this will bring you closer to certain goals. You will overcome a major problem that you have encountered and news of money will bring some happiness to your life.

January 31st, Monday

You may be feeling a little irritable and be short-tempered today. This will alter and things start to finally go your way. Certain things that you have tried to do have not turned out to be so easy in the past so this will definitely make a change. More changes at work are indicated, but this time they will be to your advantage.

FEBRUARY

February 1st, Tuesday

You may receive a letter that brings good news. This will bring happiness to your life and will give you new ideas for a project that you had given up on. You are now on the right track and progress will be made.

February 2nd, Wednesday

A wish that you have made in the past will finally come true today. You will have a better position in life from today on. Try to have a little more understanding with a family member as you may have been a little too strict with them. Listen to their views and then take the appropriate action.

February 3rd, Thursday

This will prove to be a very good day moneywise and you will be over the moon with a partner. There will be very good news on the way. You will be in a different frame of mind and will have a different attitude with a business project. Something that you hear on the radio will interest you and put you in a very good mood.

February 4th, Friday

If opportunity knocks, do not let it pass you by as you could regret it at a later date. This will also be a good time for making new business deals. What happens today will govern what happens over the next few weeks.

February 5th, Saturday

Don't be bullied into a situation that you do not really want to take part in. Stand your ground and don't move an inch as this time you are well and truly in the right. You

will win this one. It will put a smile on your face but try not to rub it in as this will only cause more friction.

February 6th, Sunday

You may need to pay a little attention to a family matter, but this is not necessarily a bad thing. It will bring many good times to your family. Plans made today will certainly come to pass and you will be closer to a personal goal.

February 7th, Monday

This will be the day that your luck changes for the better and things start to finally go your way. Certain things that you have tried to do have not turned out to be so easy in the past so this will definitely make a change. More changes at work are indicated, but this time they will be to your advantage.

February 8th, Tuesday

A travel plan may have to be changed at the last minute. However, this will turn out for the best and any time that you lose will be made up later on in the day. A work colleague may help you in more ways than one. You may find it a little odd that they are going out of their way to help you, but there may be a method in their madness. Just play along with them as you can only benefit from their helping hand.

February 9th, Wednesday

Today may turn out to be a little more hectic than you anticipated. Don't worry as this evening will be very relaxing and you will still have plenty of time to put up your feet. You should have a chat with a loved one and get certain things out into the open. It will clear the air and bring you closer to your partner.

February 10th, Thursday

A friend in need is a friend indeed, so try not to forget your friends. Planetary influences indicate that one of your friends may need a shoulder to cry on, so try to put a little time aside for them, as you never know when you might need a shoulder yourself. Go out of your way to cheer them up and you will definitely benefit from what you achieve today.

February 11th, Friday

If you are unattached, this may be the day that you meet the person of your dreams. Planetary influences indicate that your love life is about to liven up, so get ready for some action. Money matters may need some attention, but you will have no cause to worry as there is an unexpected windfall on its way.

February 12th, Saturday

You may meet a very attractive stranger and they might make a bee-line for you, but there will be more to it than meets the eye. Don't give in to flattery as they really don't mean what they say. Don't be taken in and you will not regret it. You will find out at a later date just what they were up to.

February 13th, Sunday

A loved one may get out of the wrong side of the bed, so let whatever they say fly over your head. Don't play into their hands as they may be seeking an argument. It will not help you if you go into work in a bad mood. However, a good day will be had by all and when you return home all will be forgotten.

February 14th, Monday

Don't let a family member irritate you as they are out for their own ends as they can be a little selfish. Look out for yourself today and you need to concentrate on more important matters. Luck will take a turn for the better and good news comes in a very strange way.

February 15th, Tuesday

Try not to hurt a loved one's feelings just because you don't get your own way today. It's time you gave in a little as this will not hinder your progress. You are set for many changes and will receive good news of money. Someone's good fortune will benefit you in many ways.

February 16th, Wednesday

If you go shopping today, be sure to prepare yourself for delays as planetary influences indicate that you may get held up. Don't worry as you will have better luck in the afternoon. Try not to be too tempted to part with your cash as you may be buying things that you do not really need.

February 17th, Thursday

Travel is indicated today, but if you are not travelling you may be making plans with a loved one for a holiday of a lifetime. Set the ball rolling now and you certainly will not regret it.

February 18th, Friday

You may have a lot of work to get through today but try not to overdo it. Take your time and you will get more done. A phone call that you receive today will bear good news and this will be the beginning of an exciting chapter of your life. There is news of money that is on its way. Try not to spend it before you receive it.

February 19th, Saturday

You may find it hard to concentrate and have other things on your mind. However, you must do your best not to let your imagination take over as a very important matter may pass you by. Try to keep alert. Time will pass slowly today and you may feel as if the day will never come to an end. This may not be one of your better days, but it will not turn out to be as bad as you first thought.

February 20th, Sunday

A day of rest lies ahead. Use this time to recharge your batteries. Spend time with a loved one. It will be worth your while. You may find yourself making plans to change your decor, but don't get too involved or plan to change too much. You may not find the time to carry out your plans as you will be very busy on the work front.

February 21st, Monday

A busy day lies ahead and you will certainly make good progress. A close friend will ask a favour, but you may be unable to actually help. However, good advice will be just as good. Love matters will be on your mind, but don't take any action today. You will know when the time is right to discuss matters of the heart.

February 22nd, Tuesday

Look into your heart today when you are faced with a decision. New business plans will crop up out of the blue and what happens today will govern your future. Major changes are about to happen and your life will improve tremendously.

February 23rd, Wednesday

What you hear on the grapevine will benefit you greatly if you act now. Someone may try to put you off, but take no

notice as they have their own reasons. Keep your ideas to yourself as someone may use them and benefit before you do. Secrecy is the key if you wish to advance.

February 24th, Thursday

You may be surrounded with people who take pleasure in putting people down. Take no notice as they may be feeling a little jealous of someone's success. Love matters may need a little attention. It's time that you cut down on a few of those luxuries.

February 25th, Friday

You may find yourself faced with a few problems. Don't let this get you down as you will overcome any problems that you encounter today. A loved one will be a great help and you will find out just who your real friends are.

February 26th, Saturday

You may be feeling a little low today. Try not to make any major decisions as planetary influences are clouding your thoughts. Sit this one out and you will not regret any moves that you do not make. A loved one may try to influence you to do something that you really do not want to. Do give it a try and you will enjoy the new challenge.

February 27th, Sunday

If a loved one gives you a hard time, stand up for yourself today. Don't back down as you will be in the right. If you give in, you will regret it. Stand your ground and you will overcome any problems.

February 28th, Monday

Travel is indicated today and you will get the opportunity to change the direction that you are in. Love problems will

soon change for the better and money matters that have
been on your mind will soon disappear into the distance,
never to return.

February 29th, Tuesday

Let your hair down today. Have some fun and let your work
slip into the back of your mind. Changes will come your way
and future events will please you. A good omen is starred for
today. Today's events will govern what will happen in the
near future.

MARCH

March 1st, Wednesday

Plan your day well, but don't expect things to go according to plan. Try not to panic as this will only be a temporary problem, but don't get too disappointed if you do not make any real progress today. However, it's not all doom and gloom as there will be good news when you return home. This will surprise you in more ways than one.

March 2nd, Thursday

You may feel as if there is something missing from your life, but the grass always looks greener on the other side. There is very good news on its way concerning money matters. This will allow you to really put plans into action and improve your life.

March 3rd, Friday

A letter that you receive may bring your attention to a matter that you never thought would come up at this moment in time. Don't worry as this is not as bad as it seems. It will work out for the best and will prove to bring good fortune your way, so try not to panic.

March 4th, Saturday

After the hectic week that you just have had, today's events will make you feel on top of the world and relax your mind. Don't worry about the coming week as there will be very good news and you will feel as if progress is really being made. Sit back, relax and enjoy the day and just let the world go by. Love matters take a turn for the better and an enjoyable evening lies ahead.

March 5th, Sunday

Someone from your past may get in contact with you, but do your best to get out of any meeting that they suggest as this may only bring complications to your life. At this present moment you really do not want anybody trying to confuse you. Remember, if it did not work in the past it may not work in the future, so it's best left in your past.

March 6th, Monday

If you are faced with an uncomfortable situation at work, today is the day to confront the person who may have been giving you a hard time. You must use all your tact and be as polite as possible to avoid adding to the confusion that may surround you. Share your views and get things out in the open. This will clear the air.

March 7th, Tuesday

You may find yourself in a situation that you will enjoy and a lot of fun will be had by you and all around you. Listen to what a friend has to say about a situation that you may need a little advice on, as what they have to say will make a lot of sense.

March 8th, Wednesday

Today may be a little on the hectic side, though not in the way you think, but will turn out to be one very good day. The colour blue will be very lucky for you today. Put on a smile; it will work wonders. You will find that people are attracted to you today, so use it to your own advantage. The spotlight will be on you, so put on the best show that you can and you will be surprised at the outcome.

March 9th, Thursday

You may be feeling a little on the restless side today, but you must keep your mind free from problems that you have encountered in the past as this will only bring down your good mood, so leave the past where it belongs and enjoy the day.

March 10th, Friday

You will be hearing from a family member and they will bear good news about someone whom you have not seen for a long time. You will shortly be seeing this person and this will be the beginning of a very good friendship.

March 11th, Saturday

A day of relaxation lies ahead. You will be pleased that you finally have a little peace and quiet in your home. Use this time to think about the coming week and you will be thinking crystal clear. You will also be in for a bit of a treat tonight – so be prepared for a good time.

March 12th, Sunday

You may feel a little on the down side and you may feel like throwing in the towel, but don't worry as you will be the receiver of some rather exciting news which will soon cheer you up and change your mood. Planetary influences indicate that there will be very big changes about to take place.

March 13th, Monday

You may be thinking of having a good sort-out today, but before you throw anything out have a good look at what you are about to throw out. You'll find you will save yourself time and money with what you find in the rubbish, so make sure you have a good look before you throw it out.

March 14th, Tuesday

Try to put others' feelings first before you hurt a loved one or maybe yourself. You may be in a bit of a selfish mood so try to place your own needs last, as if you do your own thing today it will only land you in trouble.

March 15th, Wednesday

A tall stranger may enter your life today. Use great caution as you will be tempted to have a little fun. By all means have fun, but try not to let this go too far. Money matters will improve and a new chapter of your life is about to begin.

March 16th, Thursday

You will feel like a new person today and will discover things about others and see the things that you turned a blind eye to. You seem to be attracting others and you may feel as if this is the wrong time to attract people as you have a lot on your mind and better things to spend your time on. Decline those offers with grace. Turn a blind eye as you are not missing out on much.

March 17th, Friday

You may have a lot on your mind and it's high time you spoke your mind. Air your thoughts with family members and friends. This is sure to clear the air. You may need to organise your life and put certain plans that you have made into action.

March 18th, Saturday

You may find yourself running around trying to get certain jobs done and not thinking about what you really should be doing. Throw down your tools, or cleaning rags or put off washing the car. Go out and have some fun. Those jobs can wait for another day.

March 19th, Sunday

If you are thinking about changing your career this may not be the time to make any changes in your life. Planetary influences indicate that bigger and better things are on their way and a better offer will come your way, so put off any major move for a little while and you certainly will not fail.

March 20th, Monday

Someone that may have done you a bad turn in the past will try to right their wrong. Don't be too hard on them as their intentions are genuine. Give them a second chance as this person will not betray you again.

March 21st, Tuesday

You may be feeling a little blue today but don't worry as it's only planetary influence doing its thing. If you are feeling a little bad-tempered try not to take it out on the wrong people as this will only add fuel to the fire. As the day progresses your mood will lift and you'll see the world for what it really is. Loved ones are set to please you, but try not to take them for granted.

March 22nd, Wednesday

This will be the perfect day to advance within your love life. Push yourself forward and you will not go far wrong. Also take extra care with a family member and keep those ideas to yourself as someone else may take all the credit. A good day will be yours, but you must use certain tactics to get through the day with ease.

March 23rd, Thursday

Listen to what others have to say today as what will you hear in a strange room will benefit you greatly. You may pick up on a good idea which will cause your life to take a different turn, but it will definitely be for the better.

March 24th, Friday

You may find yourself falling in love all over again. If you are unattached, you just could bump into your soulmate, so keep your eyes open. This will be a very lucky day for you and will prove to be more than successful.

March 25th, Saturday

Take time out today to do those jobs that desperately need doing as you may not really get the chance to do them in the near future. Be sure to sort out that paperwork too as you just may have forgotten something very important.

March 26th, Sunday

Today will be full of adventure not to mention a little romance too. You also may find yourself falling for a stranger but there is a danger that you may never see this person again so make sure you exchange names and addresses. You may not see this person for a while but they will get in contact.

March 27th, Monday

Someone on the work front may be talking rubbish. Or that may be your opinion, but pay attention as they may give you some very important information. Friends will play a big part in your life today, so be prepared for a phone call.

March 28th, Tuesday

You may have made arrangements for this evening, but you may find that certain details have changed. Don't worry as you'll find that you will have a good time. Try a new place or make extra efforts to please a loved one. This will pay big dividends.

March 29th, Wednesday

You may be thinking about taking up a hobby that you quite fancy, but you may find out that it is a little more expensive than you first thought. Try not to let the money side of the matter put you off as you will find out that it will be more than worth the money.

March 30th, Thursday

You may have a very good reason to celebrate today. Whether it's a reason of your own or someone close this will be an enjoyable day. Pop a bottle of the best or indulge in what you like best. You may find that you have far more fun than you first thought.

March 31st, Friday

You may find yourself in very strange surroundings, but this will be quite pleasurable and you will be able to relax without anybody getting on your nerves. Peace and harmony will be yours for the taking and you will have the time of your life. Get ready for some real fun.

APRIL

April 1st, Saturday

You may be feeling a little low today as someone near to you
may be having better luck, but it will soon be your turn to
advance and you will get what you want, so a little patience
is needed and it will all work out for the best.

April 2nd, Sunday

You may be delayed with a business project that surrounds
you but take this time to reorganise the situation. If
someone asks a favour try to decline as you need to pay a
little more attention to your own personal needs.

April 3rd, Monday

You may be running around in circles but you must slow
down and relax as you'll get more done in the long run.
Take care with a loved one today as they may be feeling a
little run-down. You can improve the situation by paying a
little more attention to them. This will ensure that the day
runs smoothly.

April 4th, Tuesday

Something that you have on your mind may be troubling you.
The best thing to do is to ask advice from a stranger. At least
you will get a true opinion. Take a little care whom you tell
your secrets to, as the people around you today are not very
good at keeping secrets. Tell someone whom you hardly
know and this way it will not come back via someone else.

April 5th, Wednesday

The wheel of fortune is spinning very fast. This would be a
good time to put money on the lottery or take part in a game
of chance. However, don't get too carried away as there will

only be small wins. Animals will play a large part in your life today and a recent buy will turn out better than first thought.

April 6th, Thursday

You may be surrounded by strangers today and it will be very enjoyable. You will be meeting a lot of new people and at least one will stay in your life for quite a long time. Today will have a very good end to it and you'll be more than pleased with what you accomplished.

April 7th, Friday

Don't feel low, as certain matters may be getting you down. Today will be just full of surprises. Someone will help you in more ways than one, so keep smiling as you will be contented with your situation after today is over.

April 8th, Saturday

A good day lies ahead and you will feel on top of the world. Money matters are already looking up and you can see your life getting better. Love matters are set to improve too, and what happens tonight will inspire you for the next few months.

April 9th, Sunday

Don't get yourself involved in any games of chance today. Keep your money in your purse, which is the best place for it. After today is over, planetary influences indicate that your luck will improve and a loved one will bring good news concerning a family member.

April 10th, Monday

You may need to take a new position within your working life so that you keep on top of things. You may need to make certain changes to keep up with the times, but this will ensure that you stay up there where you want to be.

April 11th, Tuesday

You will receive a surprise phone call today and what you are told will please you. Look at a problem from a distance. Things will not seem as bad as you first thought. Be careful in whom you place your trust as you may be putting your confidence in the wrong people.

April 12th, Wednesday

Listen carefully to what a loved one has to say and you will gain some insight into what the future may bring. Making plans will be very productive and everything will work out according to plan.

April 13th, Thursday

It may come to your attention that someone close may need a helping hand. This will open your eyes to a situation that you never thought would arise, but all will be well in the end. Your personal life will take a turn for the better and good news awaits you.

April 14th, Friday

You will have your eyes opened today and you may also find out just who your friends really are. Try not to look shocked as you may be turning your back on someone who you thought would be in your life for a long time. However, everything happens for a reason and you will gain a better friend.

April 15th, Saturday

A good opportunity may come your way. Before you turn it down you must look at it from all sides, both positive and negative. If it looks good, take up the offer and consider the benefits. This will be a time when you change your direction. In one way or another the result will be very productive.

April 16th, Sunday

You may find yourself in unfamiliar territory. Don't let this scare you, or at least don't let it show. You will now find that things in general may be a little hectic, but the pace will ease off and you will find that you are still on the right track.

April 17th, Monday

You may feel as if you are waiting for something to happen, or as if your life has been put on hold, but it's just that things in general are going well and you may think things are too good to be true at the moment. Try not to worry as you will not experience any setbacks. Things will run smoothly and will keep on the same even track.

April 18th, Tuesday

You may have cause for a small celebration today. You will enjoy family and friends' company. It looks as if a family outing is on the cards. This will be an eye-opener, but don't let certain matters put you off as you will have not only a good day but also a very enjoyable evening.

April 19th, Wednesday

If you are out driving today, make sure that you do not exceed the speed limits as you never know who may be on the look-out. Be extra careful as you may end up with a fine. This can be avoided if you watch your speed when driving.

April 20th, Thursday

At this present time in your life you will benefit from plans that you have made in the past. Your personal life should now be on an upward turn. Money that changes hands will be very beneficial to you in the coming months and will secure your near future.

April 21st, Friday

If you are planning to travel, this will be the perfect day to make a trip to the travel agent. Try not to let them persuade you into a cheap deal. If you take it, you will not be pleased with what you receive. Take time to think things through and you will not regret turning down a bargain.

April 22nd, Saturday

You may think that you are trapped in certain aspects of your life. However, this is far from the case as you will soon find out. Look at other people's lives before you start to criticise your own.

April 23rd, Sunday

Take time out for a loved one today as a partner may be feeling a little neglected. This will be a positive day with a positive outcome. A new chapter of your life is about to begin. It may turn out to be more than just the usual pleasant day.

April 24th, Monday

Someone's attitude may really annoy you and try your patience to the limit. It would be in your own interest to speak your mind as this person may be a little jealous of you. That is their problem so try to turn a blind eye to them.

April 25th, Tuesday

Take a good look around you and you'll be surprised at what you take for granted. You may feel a little stuck in a situation, but you'll soon move forward to better things. Try not to be impatient as you'll soon be moving into the fast lane.

April 26th, Wednesday

If you expect people to rush around and get things done, you may have a bit of a wait on your hands. Don't bank on them. The only person whom you can rely on is yourself. However, you will get through the day with ease. You will be in for a rather interesting evening and quite a treat.

April 27th, Thursday

You may have a deadline to meet. Try not to panic as you will get through and achieve it. Try not to be too hard on yourself as you deserve some congratulations. Give yourself a treat, and pamper yourself by doing something that you really enjoy doing.

April 28th, Friday

A different light will be cast on a work situation and you'll be very surprised at what the outcome will be. To your surprise it will work out to your advantage. Don't worry over money matters as your purse will be full, but unfortunately not bottomless. Spend your money with care.

April 29th, Saturday

You may find that you are in new surroundings and in new company. Your personality may not be coming through as you may be feeling a little shy. Push yourself forward and you'll soon be the centre of attention. Try not to show off as you may give someone the wrong impression.

April 30th, Sunday

You'll probably be very pleased that the month is nearly over, as it has been a bit hectic, but better times lie directly ahead and you will be all the wiser for what you have been through. Get ready for a good month as the coming month will bring new directions and happiness into your life.

MAY

May 1st, Monday

You should really put your heart and soul into your work today as you will have the opportunity to better your position and get the right people on your side at the right time. You may advance to heights that you never thought possible whether at home or at work. Whatever you are involved in, make sure that you do your best.

May 2nd, Tuesday

Today will prove to be full of fun and adventure. You will also learn alot about the people you spend time with today, which could influence many decisions you make in the future. Remember all you learn today as it will prove to be a very important time.

May 3rd, Wednesday

Don't rely on electrical items today as this may be a day when the things that you use the most let you down. This goes for people too, so try to manage without either. If you need some advice on your career, you may need to speak to someone who has no experience in that field. You may need to have a little break and time to yourself.

May 4th, Thursday

It's a new day with a new direction. You will be more than pleased with what happens today and will certainly be in for a treat. You will find that a happy atmosphere surrounds you and that you will receive good news. It may be something that you have been waiting for, but try not to get over-excited as you may tire yourself out.

May 5th, Friday

Your life will get a little hectic and you'll be in real demand and you have to spread yourself out very thin, so make sure there is enough to go around. Take time to listen to what friends have to say or you may be in danger of missing a good opportunity.

May 6th, Saturday

You may feel an inner loneliness today, but don't worry as help is at hand. Someone, whom you didn't expect to, will come to your rescue with useful advice. When you have heard the advice you will know which direction to take. This will ensure that you are heading for a better future

May 7th, Sunday

If you are worrying over a family matter, you will be pleased to know that the problem will soon be solved and all your worries will be over. Try not to waste your time worrying over things that may never happen.

May 8th, Monday

Someone from your past may walk back into your life. You should not take what they tell you to heart as they may have their own reasons for getting in contact with you again. Be sure not to commit yourself to them as you will not have enough time for them in the future.

May 9th, Tuesday

You may be in two minds about what to do regarding love matters. You may feel like walking away from your current partner, but would you be doing the right thing? It would not be wise to act on impulse. Take a break and have a good think before you act. Your mind will then be clearer and you will know exactly what to do.

May 10th, Wednesday

You will have the opportunity to rid yourself of something that you have wanted to get out of your life. Once you sort things out you will never look back and definitely not have any regrets. You will find that certain events that are taking place are working out very well.

May 11th, Thursday

Make your views clear to a partner or family member as they may expect a little more than you can give at the moment. You may be very tired of the arguments that surround you, but the air will be cleared very soon and nobody will be left in the dark. Then you will know just where everybody stands and the problem will be resolved.

May 12th, Friday

If you have a secret, now is the right time to share it. A loved one or close friend will be amused with your story and at the same time you will get things off your chest.

May 13th, Saturday

You may feel like going on a shopping spree today. This will do you a world of good. You may feel like treating yourself and why not? After all, you deserve it.

May 14th, Sunday

You will hear news that you will receive some money, but try not to spend it before you actually receive it. It may take a little longer to reach your bank account than you anticipate. However, it will come in the end and you'll have less cause for worry.

May 15th, Monday

You may see something that you want to buy and now would be the right time to buy it. Listen to yourself for once and do what you really want to do. You'll certainly be pleased with what your lover or friends think. Go on, treat yourself. You only live once.

May 16th, Tuesday

You will have a change of mind about the direction that you would like your life to take. Try not to be too quick to change certain matters as your life is set to change for the better of its own accord.

May 17th, Wednesday

Today may pass very quickly and you may wonder just where the time went. However, you may also find that you have managed to get a lot done. Planetary influences indicate that you will be the receiver of some very good news.

May 18th, Thursday

You can make a difference to your life if you put your mind to it, but you may need a little push now and again. It's high time you started to push yourself forward a little of your own accord. After all, you do not really want someone else to take the credit for your actions.

May 19th, Friday

Listen to your heart today. You may feel the need to change direction, but you just don't know where to start. You must take one day at a time and, if it's to be, then you will certainly go in the direction that you wish. A new door and chapter of your life will open.

May 20th, Saturday

Someone may be on your mind. If you are worried, pick up the phone and give them a call. You'll soon find out that everything is OK and that you are just a born worrier. You'll be surprised at just how well things are going. At least this will put your mind at rest.

May 21st, Sunday

You may be running late today with certain commitments. Don't worry as when you put your mind to it you will certainly catch up and you'll get more done than you think.

May 22nd, Monday

You may feel as if there should be something more to life and you may feel at a low. However, you should take a good look around you and you will realise that you are just feeling a little negative today. Your life will soon change of its own accord and you will be pleased with the outcome of your present situation. You will also be very pleased that you did not make any hasty decisions.

May 23rd, Tuesday

You may be quick to judge a stranger today, but you should give them the benefit of the doubt. You may find that you have judged them wrongly. This person may turn out to be totally different from what you first thought.

May 24th, Wednesday

It may start off as just another routine Wednesday, but you may meet a complete stranger whom you will feel you have known all your life. No doubt you will stay good friends for a long time.

May 25th, Thursday

Your life should now be moving into the fast lane and you may find that it may be a little too fast for you. However, it will not remain at such a high pace and will slow down to a more comfortable speed. You should expect to make new friends and move on to higher ground.

May 26th, Friday

You may be feeling guilty about money that you have recently spent. There is no point in crying over spilt milk. Don't worry as you will get through with flying colours as money will come to you from an unexpected source.

May 27th, Saturday

Today will prove to be more than successful and you'll find out that you will be on the receiving end of some very good news. News about money matters will come to your attention and you will be planning to have a celebration in the near future.

May 28th, Sunday

A shopping spree may be on the cards today. Try not to go overboard as you may find you will go over budget. You must cut down a little as you will need the money at a later date. Try to put a little to one side for a rainy day.

May 29th, Monday

You may receive a phone call with very good news. A business proposition may be put to you. Give some serious thought before you enter any new ventures as you may already have taken on too much. You may need to pay a little attention to your finances before they get out of hand. Any problems that you discover now will be sorted out and this will be of benefit to you in the near future.

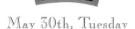

May 30th, Tuesday

If you have had the past on your mind this may give you inspiration for the future. You will not make the same mistake twice. You may be thinking too seriously about the situation that you are in. Good will come from today and your luck is about to change.

May 31st, Wednesday

Today may prove to be rather a mystifying day. You must keep an open mind and you will be wiser after today's events. Try not to be tempted to spend any money as you will find that you have wasted it. The colour green will be good luck for you today.

JUNE

June 1st, Thursday

Today will be the start of an adventure that will unravel slowly. All will be revealed, so try to be patient. Love matters are coming close to a head and you should take a family member's advice. Try not to be wooed into a situation that you will not benefit by as you may be wasting your time. A change of direction is needed. Act today and make a start with something that you have planned. You will not regret it.

June 2nd, Friday

A family member may need your full attention. Any mishaps that have occurred in your family will right themselves today. You will receive some good news and news of travel will come your way. A stranger whom you meet in the street will give you insight into your future. You may come across this person again, so take notice of them.

June 3rd, Saturday

Look deeply into your heart and you will find the direction that you need to get you through the day. Don't listen to small talk and certainly don't take seriously any promises that are made today as they may be broken. If you need to get things done, I suggest that you do them yourself today. You cannot go wrong then, and you will not suffer any setbacks.

June 4th, Sunday

You may feel a little puzzled over a loved one's action but don't worry as this will only be a passing phase. Try to look on the brighter side of life today as you will need to put yourself in a good frame of mind for the treat tonight.

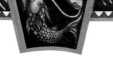

June 5th, Monday

You will be pleased that today will turn out to be a very successful day. You will make great headway with any matters that you have been putting off. You will receive good news concerning money matters. Love and contentment will surround you and your mind will be at peace.

June 6th, Tuesday

A letter that you receive today will give you peace of mind. If you are worrying about a family matter, try not to think too deeply as you may be worrying over something that may never come off. News of travel will come to your attention and plans that you make now will save you time in the near future.

June 7th, Wednesday

Spend time with friends and family as this will be a day to remember. You may receive an invitation to a small party. You should consider this with care before you accept the offer. You may bump into someone whom you have not seen for some time. This may add a little spark to your life, but try not to get too close to the flame as you just may get your fingers burned.

June 8th, Thursday

Your business life will take a turn for the better today. You may need to back-track and go over some of your past before you make further progress. Money matters that have been on your mind will improve and good news comes from a family member. This will improve your life and bring much happiness.

June 9th, Friday

You may feel as if you are in limbo today with certain aspects of your life. You may get extra inspiration from your immediate surroundings. This will give you some ideas. If

you have planned travel or a business move, now is the time to get the ball rolling as planetary influences indicate that luck will be on your side.

June 10th, Saturday

If someone has fallen out with you for no apparent reason in the past, you just may find out today the real reason why. However, don't let the past hinder your future. New friends will be made and you will find out just who is who. Real friends will be made and this will be the start of an exciting new chapter of your life.

June 11th, Sunday

Your life will return to normal today. Planetary influences have hindered you and held you back a little, but the way ahead is clear. You may find that your life is finally moving forward and exciting matters are about to come to a head. You are about to move into the fast lane. Get ready for the ride of a lifetime. You will not forget it in a hurry.

June 12th, Monday

You may receive a very good offer today, but watch out as it may be too good to be true. Try not to add to your workload as you may have too much on your plate already. Slow down a little before you become completely worn out. If you feel a little low, try a herbal remedy. A little relaxation will do you a world of good or maybe it is time to give yourself a treat.

June 13th, Tuesday

Someone who wears red will bring you good luck. A major change is foreseen and a stranger brings money closer to your bank account. You may advance in ways that you never thought possible and success is within your grasp.

June 14th, Wednesday

A phone call that you receive today will please you greatly. Family problems that you have encountered will be resolved and new foundations will be laid. You must speak your mind to a loved one, as rules laid down now will save time and trouble at a later date. Try to put money aside for some fun as you will soon get the opportunity to better your life.

June 15th, Thursday

Temptation may stand in your way today. Look before you leap, as this situation may be a lot of fun but it may complicate your life and add to your stress. You could do without this at the moment. You may just get caught in the act which would do more harm than good to a relationship. You must decline any offer at all costs as there will be a better opportunity at a later date.

June 16th, Friday

Take time out to have a little fun. Try going somewhere that you have never been before. A shopping spree may be the answer. You may have had your eye on that certain something for some time now. This is the right time to treat yourself. You deserve it. Money matters will improve and a better position within a work situation is foreseen.

June 17th, Saturday

This will be a rewarding day, but try now to rely on others too much as they may let you down. It is best to rely on your own abilities and resources. Someone from the past will get in touch soon, so try to put some time to one side for old times' sake. It will be worth your while.

June 18th, Sunday

Something that you have wanted in the past will be within your reach now. You may be a little undecided about just which direction to take, but follow your instincts and you won't go far wrong. Don't be influenced by others.

June 19th, Monday

You may have to throw yourself in at the deep end with a business matter before you make any headway. This will be a day when you really get things done and you will get a project off the ground. The ball will start to roll and you will reap big rewards. Don't hesitate. Go for it.

June 20th, Tuesday

You may ask yourself where you go from here. However, just as you are feeling that the situation has no future, a new opportunity will appear right before your eyes. You must not give in to a negative frame of mind as this will do you no good. You must be positive or something good may just pass you by.

June 21st, Wednesday

You may be faced with an awkward situation today, but you must use caution and choose your words with care as the person whom you will be dealing with may just be feeling a little delicate. You will make progress and this situation will go your way. The number 6 will be lucky and someone with a 6 in their date of birth will bring changes for the better to your life.

June 22nd, Thursday

You may have the urge to take up some sort of sport or put a keep-fit plan together. This will do no harm and you will benefit by it if you stick to your plans. A new idea may spring into your head. Put it down on paper as it will result in many good things and open many new doors to you in the near future.

June 23rd, Friday

Someone may really get your back up today, but at all costs try not to play into their hands as you may just regret airing your feelings. Try to keep them to yourself. It will be the best policy. Turn the other cheek and you will win the day. Plans that you have made in the past will start to come into action and a good atmosphere will now surround you.

June 24th, Saturday

You will have a strange meeting with someone whom you find very attractive. You must resist any temptation at all cost as you may find yourself in a very awkward situation which may do damage to an existing relationship.

June 25th, Sunday

You may be feeling a little irritable and you may have a short fuse today. However, as the day progresses this feeling will fade away into the distance and not return for some time. A chance meeting with an old friend is starred and money matters will improve.

June 26th, Monday

You may receive a letter that brings good news. This will bring happiness into your life and will give you extra inspiration for a project that you had given up on. You are now on the right track and progress will be made.

June 27th, Tuesday

An ambition will be realised today which will please you immensely. You will have a better position in life from today on. Try to have a little more patience with a family member as you may have been a little to hard on them in the past. Hear them out and then take the appropriate action.

June 28th, Wednesday

This will prove to be a very prosperous day and you will be over the moon with a partner as there will be very good news on the way. You will be in a different frame of mind and will have a different attitude with a business project. Something which you hear on the radio will inspire you and put you in a very good mood.

June 29th, Thursday

If opportunity knocks, do not let this pass you by. You may regret this at a later date. This will also be a good time for making new business deals. What happens today will influence what happens over the next few weeks.

June 30th, Friday

Don't be bullied into a situation that you do not really want to be involved in. Stand your ground and don't move an inch, as this time you are well and truly in the right. You will win this one and it will put a smile on your face. However, try not to rub it in as it will only cause more friction.

JULY

July 1st, Saturday

You may need to pay a little attention to a family matter, but this is not necessarily a bad thing. It will bring many good times to your family. Plans made today will definitely come to pass and you will be closer to a personal goal.

July 2nd, Sunday

You may find yourself running around in circles, but this will do you no good at all. You must try to stay calm and you will get more done. You will overcome any obstacles that try to stand in your way. It really is the perfect day to get ahead with any household chores. Love is starred well and it looks as if you are in for a bit of a treat tonight.

July 3rd, Monday

This will be the day that your luck changes for the better and things finally start to go your way. Certain things that you have tried to do have not been so easy in the past. This will definitely make a change. More changes at work are indicated, but this time they will be to your advantage.

July 4th, Tuesday

A travel plan may have to be changed at the last minute, but this will turn out for the best and time that you lose will be made up later on in the day. A work colleague may help you in more ways than one. You may find it a little odd that they are going out of their way to help you. There may be a method in their madness, but just play along with them as you can only benefit from their helping hand.

July 5th, Wednesday

You may feel like a change of scene. It may come to your attention just how much you have neglected certain people and most of all someone whom you hold very close to your heart. However, all is not lost and you can correct this if you take action now. Pay some attention to those whom you have forgotten.

July 6th, Thursday

Listen to your heart today when you are faced with a decision. New business plans will spring up out of the blue and the events of today will govern your future. Major changes are about to take place and your life will improve tremendously.

July 7th, Friday

What you hear on the grapevine will benefit you greatly if you act now. Someone may try to put you off, but take no notice as they have their own agenda. Keep your ideas to yourself as someone may use your ideas and benefit from them before you do. Secrecy is the key if you wish to advance.

July 8th, Saturday

You may stumble upon another person's secret today, which will prove to be very opportune. Some idle gossip will give you the information that you have needed. Use this information to your own advantage, but try not to mention it as someone may just try to steal your ideas. Keep your success to yourself for a little while.

July 9th, Sunday

You may find that you are faced with a rather exciting challenge today. What you previously thought impossible in the past will now start to be within your reach. However, you will be very pleased with the result of today's events. Many new doors will open and problems that you have encountered will be solved.

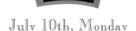

July 10th, Monday

You may be feeling a little low today. Try not to make any major decisions as planetary influences are clouding your thoughts. Sit this one out and you will not regret moves that you have not made. A loved one may try to influence you to do something that you really do not want to do, but give it a try. You will enjoy this new experience.

July 11th, Tuesday

You may be thinking about having a relaxing day, but be prepared for someone to knock on your door. If you don't really feel like guests, don't answer the door or you may have your day taken up by someone whom you have no time for.

July 12th, Wednesday

If a loved one gives you a hard time, stand up for yourself today. Don't back down as you will be in the right. If you give in you will regret it. Stand your ground and you will overcome any problems.

July 13th, Thursday

Travel is indicated today and you will get the opportunity to change the direction that you are in. Love problems that you have encountered will soon change for the better and money matters that have been on your mind will soon disappear into the distance, never to return.

July 14th, Friday

Someone close may need a helping hand today. You may feel that this has come at a very inconvenient time, but everything happens for a reason. Try to be patient and good will come from this. The situation will soon take a turn for the better.

July 15th, Saturday

You may have neglected certain aspects of your life and this will need some sort of attention. Take care before you plan on spending money on extravagant items. Use caution before parting with any hard-earned cash. Make plans to improve your home, but make sure that you cover all possibilities.

July 16th, Sunday

A work situation that you have not made any real headway with will start to move ahead. This will please you and take a little stress out of your life. A move or a change in direction is foreseen. This will bring happiness into your life. It is also a good time to meet a new love or rekindle an old flame. A new adventure within your love life is set to happen.

July 17th, Monday

Today will prove to be successful in many ways. It will be a perfect day to change certain matters in your life that need dealing with. Use any opportunity to discuss matters with a loved one. Your luck is set to change for the better and better times lie directly ahead.

July 18th, Tuesday

You may feel as if you just want your own company, but you may prove to be your own worst enemy if you find time to spend on your own. People will only stop you from doing just what you really want to do, so speak your mind and try not to do things just to please others. It would be in your own interest if you just do your own thing today. You may need time to sort certain things out, so go it alone today. It's just what you need.

July 19th, Wednesday

You may feel like a bear with a sore head this morning. This mood will soon pass and good progress will be made. You may be in for a bit of a surprise. You may find yourself planning something that you would not normally do, but you'll be in for a good time and it will work out the way you want it to. Go full steam ahead and don't let anybody try to change your mind.

July 20th, Thursday

If you have been faced with an uncomfortable situation at work, today is the day to confront the person who may have been causing you problems. You must use tact and be as polite as possible to avoid adding to the confusion that may surround you. Share your views and get things out in the open. This will clear the air.

July 21st, Friday

You may find yourself in a situation that you will enjoy and a lot of fun will be had by you and all around you. Listen to what a friend has to say about a situation that you may need a little advice on, as what they have to tell you will make a lot of sense.

July 22nd, Saturday

Today may be a little hectic, but not in the way you imagine. It will turn out to be a very special day. The colour green will be very lucky for you today. Put on a smile; it will work wonders at work. You will find that people are attracted to you today, so use it to your own advantage. The spotlight will be on you, so put on the best show that you can and you will be surprised at the outcome.

July 23rd, Sunday

A letter that you receive today will please you greatly and it will open a door which you will want to go through. You may

find that friends will get in contact with you today. They may be planning to have a really good night out. Help make the plans and don't forget to put the date in your diary.

July 24th, Monday

Someone who thinks they can take you for granted may find out just how mistaken they are today. Stand your ground and don't do anything that you don't think fitting. Today you just may find out a few truths about certain people, but you must take this information with a pinch of salt. You can do without any more problems in your personal life.

July 25th, Tuesday

You may find yourself in unfamiliar surroundings today and a family outing is foreseen. Take care with your cash as you will be very tempted to spend it. A family member may try your patience, but at all costs try not to lose your temper with them as it will only make matters worse.

July 26th, Wednesday

You may be told a secret today, but try not to repeat it as it's only gossip and there will be no truth in it. If you repeat it, you will only be passing on misleading information, so keep it to yourself for a while. The truth will soon come into the open and clear all the rumours that may be flying around.

July 27th, Thursday

Someone may offer their advice today, but it may be very misleading and will probably be for their own purpose. It would be in your own interest to stick to your own advice today. Love problems that you have recently encountered will change for the better and you will have less to worry about.

July 28th, Friday

Beware of getting yourself into a situation that will not be easy to get out of. Think carefully before you take action as you may regret the outcome. Under no circumstance let your heart rule your head as you stand to lose more than you will gain.

July 29th, Saturday

If you have been thinking about embarking on a new venture, then this is not the day to start it. You need to sit back, relax and let the day slip by. Your loved one may need a little attention. Any time spent with a loved one will be time well spent.

July 30th, Sunday

You may be burning the candle at both ends. It may be time to slow down a little. You will need all the rest that you can get as your life will soon be entering the fast lane. This will bring a lot of exciting challenges in your life. Loved ones will be proud of what you are doing as you are set for success.

July 31st, Monday

Keep your eyes open today as there will be a bargain to be had. This will be the time to spend those pounds and you will certainly get value for money. Spend a little on your loved one. This will give you not only peace of mind but less hassle in the near future.

AUGUST

August 1st, Tuesday

You may have a lot on your mind and it's high time that you spoke your mind. Share your thoughts with family members and friends. This is sure to clear the air. You may need to organise your life and put certain plans that you have made into action.

August 2nd, Wednesday

You may find yourself running around trying to get certain jobs done and not thinking about what you really should be doing. Leave any unnecessary chores until later. Go out and have some fun. Those jobs can wait for another day.

August 3rd, Thursday

If you have been thinking about changing your career, this may be the wrong time to make any changes. Planetary influences indicate that bigger and better things are on their way and a better offer will come your way. So just be patient for a little while and you certainly will not fail.

August 4th, Friday

Someone who may have done you a bad turn in the past will try to right their wrong. Don't be too hard on them as their intentions are genuine. Give them a second chance and they will not betray you again.

August 5th, Saturday

You may be feeling a little blue today, but don't worry as it's only the result of planetary influences. If you are feeling a little bad-tempered try not to take it out on innocent people as this will only add fuel to the fire. As the day progresses your mood will lift and you'll see the world for what it really is. Loved ones are set to please you, but try not to take them for granted.

August 6th, Sunday

If you have planned a day out, it will certainly turn out to a very good day. Be sure to take time out to make a loved one feel special as this will keep you in their good books and you can use today to lay down foundations for your future. Plan with care, but be sure you ask a loved one what their views are or you could cause an argument.

August 7th, Monday

Money matters may need sorting out and this would be the perfect day to do so. It may also be time to think about a new bank account or maybe a savings plan. A close friend will be close by to advise you on certain matters. Love looks promising today and you'll be the centre of attention tonight.

August 8th, Tuesday

This may be a good day to find out certain things that you have wanted to know but did not like to ask for fear of rocking the boat. However, this is the day to find out and you'll be thrilled with what you discover. There is news of money that may come your way, but try not to spend it before you receive it.

August 9th, Wednesday

You may find that certain aspects of your life are changing, but everything happens for a reason and you will be pleased with the changes that are taking place. You will hear news about someone from your past, but it would not be to your advantage to try to get in touch with them. Let sleeping dogs lie.

August 10th, Thursday

You will be faced with changes on the work front today but don't let this put you off as it will work out to your

advantage in the long run. Pay attention to detail as this will come in quite handy at a later date. Someone may try to put you off accepting a certain offer that you have received, but try to use your own judgement.

August 11th, Friday

You may be faced with a task that you may think impossible, but give it a go and you'll be surprised just what you can do when you put your mind to it. Someone close will certainly be proud of you and this will add to the smart image that you have. A friend will bring news of someone from your past, but it may not be what you think. You will be in for a surprise as someone may try to walk back into your life.

August 12th, Saturday

Today will be full of surprises. There will be a lot of twists and turns, but it will be a day that will certainly grab your attention. This afternoon will give you the chance to get your own back on someone and you certainly will have the last laugh.

August 13th, Sunday

What you see on TV will influence you greatly and give you inspiration for a future project. However, you must find time to relax as you have had a hectic week. News will come from a close family member and you may have to change some of your plans.

August 14th, Monday

If a loved one is a little sharp with you today, you must not rise to their remarks as this will only add fuel to the fire. It would be to your advantage to try to ignore what they say and then you'll find out just what is really irritating them.

August 15th, Tuesday

You may have a very good reason to celebrate today. Whether it's on your own account or for someone close, this will be an enjoyable day. Open a bottle of the best or indulge in a favourite drink. You may find that you have far more fun than you first thought.

August 16th, Wednesday

You may find that you have the blues and, after all that excitement yesterday, you find it very hard to concentrate. However, you must do your best as you should try not to let other matters slip. You should be ahead with your work and finally be making progress.

August 17th, Thursday

You may be feeling a little low today as someone near to you may be having better luck than you are. It will soon be your turn to do well and you will get what you want. A little patience is needed and all will work out for the best.

August 18th, Friday

You may be delayed with a business project that you are involved in, but take this time to reorganise the situation. If someone asks a favour of you, try to decline as you need to pay a little more time and attention to your own personal needs.

August 19th, Saturday

You may be running around in circles, but you must slow down and relax as you'll get more done in the long run. Take care with a loved one today as they may be feeling a little run-down. You can improve the situation by paying a little more attention to them. This will ensure that the day runs smoothly.

August 20th, Sunday

Today will be full of surprises and planetary influences indicate that your love life will improve in more ways than one. You will feel better not only with your present situation but mentally and physically, too.

August 21st, Monday

Today marks a turning point in your life. Your life is about to change in many ways and you'll be more than pleased with what is about to take place. You will improve your position and your personal life will also take a turn for the better.

August 22nd, Tuesday

Today holds the key to a secret and you'll certainly find out the answer to some of your questions. After today is over you will no longer be in the dark. Look towards the better things in life and try to be positive today and you will overcome any problems that come your way.

August 23rd, Wednesday

You may be surrounded by strangers today and you will find it very enjoyable. You will be meeting a lot of new people and at least one will stay in your life for quite a long time. Today will have a very unusual twist and you'll be more than pleased with what is accomplished.

August 24th, Thursday

Don't feel low. Certain matters may be getting you down, but today will be just full of surprises. Someone will help you in more ways than one, so keep smiling. You will be contented with your situation after today is over.

August 25th, Friday

A good day lies ahead and you will feel on top of the world. Money matters are already improving and you can see that your life is on the up and up. Love matters are set to improve, too, and what happens tonight will inspire you for the next few months.

August 26th, Saturday

If you remember a vivid dream when you wake up, be sure to put it down on paper. What lies in your dreams will have a certain meaning in the near future. However, the meaning will not be obvious at first.

August 27th, Sunday

You may be feeling a little tired of the company around you, but new people will influence you and your life will take a turn for the better on the work front. Your personal life will greatly improve and you will be moving in different circles.

August 28th, Monday

Your life is now heading in the right direction, so try not to be too keen to make a lot of changes. Think things through before making any hasty decisions and this will ensure no mistakes are made.

August 29th, Tuesday

You have been keeping a secret from a loved one. It is maybe time to come clean and this will be the perfect time to do so. This will surely clear the air and make room for future events. Something that you have been wanting will come into your possession today and will make life a little more pleasant. Others will look on with envy.

August 30th, Wednesday

You may think that a work colleague is being unreasonable today and you will not be far wrong. Try your best to keep calm and things will not get out of hand. Put it down to experience and move on things will have returned to normal by tomorrow.

August 31st, Thursday

You may be out hunting for bargains and you'll definitely find them today. You will be surrounded by a lot of choice, but you may feel confused about exactly what you want to buy. Have a good look around before you part with any cash as you never know what is around the next corner.

SEPTEMBER

September 1st, Friday

You may feel as if you are missing something, but try not to look in the wrong places. You may end up with more than you have bargained for. You may be a little vulnerable and you must get yourself out of this situation.

September 2nd, Saturday

You may have cause for a small celebration today. You will enjoy family and friends' company today. It looks as if a family outing is on the cards. This will be an eye-opener, but don't let certain matters put you off as you will have not only a good day but also a very enjoyable evening.

September 3rd, Sunday

You may find yourself in unfamiliar territory. Don't let this disturb you, or at least don't let it show if it does. You will now find that things in general may be a little on the hectic side, but they will ease off and you will find out that you are on the right track.

September 4th, Monday

Planetary influences indicate that you will receive a good turn in your life. You will be feeling better and more comfortable in your present situation. The working side of your life looks very promising and you will not regret any changes that you make now.

September 5th, Tuesday

If you are driving today, stay within the limits of the law. Be extra careful or you may end up with a fine. Take your time, even if you are late for an appointment, as this may be the undoing of a clean driving licence.

September 6th, Wednesday

At this time in your life you will benefit from plans that you have made in the past. Your personal life should now be on an upward turn. Money that changes hands will be very beneficial to you in the coming months and secure your future.

September 7th, Thursday

If you are planning a holiday, this will be the perfect time to take a trip to the travel agent. Try not to let them push you into a cheap deal as you will not be happy with it if you take it. Take time to think things through and you will not regret turning a bargain down.

September 8th, Friday

You may think that you are a little tied in certain aspects of your life, but this is far from the truth, You will find that your situation will be set to improve in the near future. Look at other people's lives before you start to criticise your own.

September 9th, Saturday

Take time out for a loved one today as a partner may be feeling a little neglected. This will be a positive day with a positive outcome. A new chapter in your life is about to begin. It may turn out to be a very unusual day.

September 10th, Sunday

Someone's attitude may really annoy you and try your patience. It would be in your own interest to speak your mind as this person may be a little jealous of you. That is their problem so speak your mind and then try to turn a blind eye.

September 11th, Monday

Someone may be eager to criticise you today, but let their words fly over your head. You must not play into their hands. Love matters may need some attention and you will find that you may have been missing out on certain matters.

September 12th, Tuesday

You will be amazed at just what takes place today. You will be over the moon with the news that you receive. A letter that you receive today may unsettle you, but this will be sorted out in a very short space of time. A loved one comes to your rescue and all will be well.

September 13th, Wednesday

Someone may try to take advantage of you. Don't let them. You will see straight through them and you should use this situation to obtain the information that you need. Let them down gently.

September 14th, Thursday

Look back into your past and try to remember the good times. This will put you in a good mood. You will need to be at your best and on top form today in order to give a good impression to someone in power who could help you in the near future. Advancement is foreseen and you will be offered a better position or a different way of earning your living.

September 15th, Friday

Love matters really play a major part in your life today and will work out to suit you. You should stick to any major decisions that you have made recently. You may also feel that you are not advancing in the way that you wish. However, your life will soon speed up in the right areas.

September 16th, Saturday

You may be missing out today if you don't keep your eyes open as something very good will come your way. Try not to let it pass you by. Someone may be trying to get your attention. It would be to your advantage to show them some interest as this will help you advance.

September 17th, Sunday

You may be very undecided today over something that you want to buy. If you are not sure, don't buy it as it may not be as useful as you think. So before you part with your money, test it out thoroughly as you don't want to be stuck with a white elephant.

September 18th, Monday

You may feel like backing out of a situation that you are in. Try not to give in too soon as you may be in a different frame of mind tomorrow. Love matters may be getting you down and adding to your problems, but if you look at your life closely things are not as bad as you make out. In certain ways you are lucky and you will come to realise this at the end of the day.

September 19th, Tuesday

What a day this will be. It will start off rather strangely and will continue to be unpredictable throughout the day. Let your hair down as you'll need a rather casual approach today. The day will run very smoothly and you'll be in a good frame of mind. It will be a good day if you are dealing with people.

September 20th, Wednesday

If you find out a home truth today, don't act on impulse as you may have got hold of the wrong end of the stick. Find out all the facts before you take any action. The phone may

ring and, although you may not be interested in the person on the other end of the line, listen to their conversation as they may just have some news which will cast a different light on your situation.

September 21st, Thursday

You may feel quite alone today but don't worry as help is at hand. Someone whom you didn't expect to give you advice comes to the rescue. After you receive this good advice you will know which direction to take. This will ensure that you are on the right road for a better future.

September 22nd, Friday

You may get some unexpected news today. Don't act on it immediately as there may be more to it than you first thought. Check the facts thoroughly. This evening there will be a chance for some fun with your friends.

September 23rd, Saturday

Planetary influences indicate that new people are about to enter your life and they will open many new doors for you. New friends will be made too and with new friends comes new money. This will make your life less complicated and ensure that you will have no more setbacks.

September 24th, Sunday

You may be faced with a very unusual situation and may not know just what to do for the best, but at the last second it will all work out. You'll certainly be thankful to be rid of the situation that you got yourself into, but now you are in the clear to do better for yourself. You will be amazed with just what is around the corner.

September 25th, Monday

You may be having a disagreement with a loved one. Try not to say things that you don't really mean as you may regret hurting your loved one's feelings. Try to calm the situation down and you'll find that it will soon be over and happiness will return to your life.

September 26th, Tuesday

You may be in two minds about what to do about love matters. You may feel like walking away from an existing partner, but would you be doing the right thing? It would not be wise to act on impulse. Take a break and have a good think before you act. Your mind will then be clearer and you will know exactly what to do.

September 27th, Wednesday

You may have had a strange dream last night, but try not to let this disturb you. Nothing bad is about to happen, so sit back, put those feet up and relax. After all, you deserve it. You will be satisfied that you have tackled a difficult task.

September 28th, Thursday

Make your thoughts clear to a partner or family member as they may expect a little more than you can give at the moment. You may be very tired of the arguments that surround you, but the air will be cleared very soon. You will then know just where everybody stands and the problem will be resolved.

September 29th, Friday

If you have a secret, now is the right time to share it. A loved one or close friend will be amused with your story and at the same time you will get things off your chest.

September 30th, Saturday

You may think that today will be no different from the rest but, to your surprise, today will turn out to be very exciting and will bring more than you ever expected. This will be the beginning of not only a new friendship but a whole new direction.

OCTOBER

October 1st, Sunday

A family member will bring very good news and there may be plans to have a celebration. This may come at a very inconvenient time, but try to put a little time aside to join in with the family fun. You won't regret it.

October 2nd, Monday

You may be in a little bit of a bad mood today but as the day progresses this mood will lift and you will then see the funny side of things. This is a good day for trying to get hold of people that are rather hard to obtain and it will also prove to be a day where you really get things done.

October 3rd, Tuesday

You may feel a little worried over a long-standing family problem, but all will be resolved and sooner than you think. You must try not to worry so much as this does not help your situation, but you will be pleased to know you will encounter better luck and money matters are set to improve.

October 4th, Wednesday

You will have a change of mind about the direction in which your life is currently running, but try not to be too fast to change certain matters as your life is set to change for the better of its own accord.

October 5th, Thursday

Today may pass very quickly and you may wonder just where the time went, but you also may find that you have managed to get a lot done. Planetary influences indicate that you will be the receiver of some very good news.

October 6th, Friday

Someone around you may think they have everything in control, but you may just be in the right place at the right time as you will be able to step in and save the day. You will receive praise and this will put you back in the spotlight.

October 7th, Saturday

You may have to let something go and you may feel as if you are taking a step back but really you are taking a step forward. This loss will be a blessing in disguise and you will soon feel at home with the changes that you just have encountered.

October 8th, Sunday

Listen to your heart today. You may feel the need to head in a new direction, but you just don't know where to start. But you must take one day at a time and, if it's to be, then you'll certainly go in the direction that you wish and a new chapter of your life will open.

October 9th, Monday

Someone may be on your mind. If you are worried, pick up the phone and give them a call. You'll soon find out that everything is OK and you are just a natural worrier and you'll be surprised just how well things are going. At least this will put your mind at rest.

October 10th, Tuesday

You may be running late today with certain matters in your life. Don't worry as when you put your mind to it you will certainly catch up and you'll get more done than you think.

October 11th, Wednesday

You may feel as if there is something better out there and you may feel at a low, but you should take a good look

around you as you are a little on the negative side today. Your life will soon change of its own accord and you will be pleased with the outcome of your present situation and you will also be very pleased that you did not make any hasty decisions.

October 12th, Thursday

A new door will open today, but you may ponder or be hesitant as to which direction you should take. You will just know deep down which is the right direction to take.

October 13th, Friday

You may be quick to judge a stranger today, but you must give them the benefit of the doubt. You may find that you have judged them wrongly and this person will turn out to be quite different from what you first thought.

October 14th, Saturday

You may meet a complete stranger whom you will feel as if you have known all your life. No doubt you will stay good friends for a long time. A fun evening out is on the cards.

October 15th, Sunday

You may be delayed with a business project that you are involved in, but take this time to reorganise the situation. If someone asks a favour of you, try to decline as you need to pay a little more attention to your own personal needs.

October 16th, Monday

Good news will land on your doorstep today. This will put you in a different frame of mind. You will feel more contented after today has passed and happiness will lie at your feet.

October 17th, Tuesday

You may think that a loved one is being contrary today. Try your best to keep your cool and things will not get out of hand. It may be a good idea to avoid them as much as possible as whatever you say will not be right. Take time-out when you return things will have reverted to their harmonious state.

October 18th, Wednesday

You may find out just who your friends really are today. However, try not to look shocked at any revelations that people make. You may be turning your back on someone whom you thought would be in your life for a long time. Everything happens for a reason and you will gain a better friend.

October 19th, Thursday

You may feel as if something is missing, but try not to look in the wrong places. You may end up with more than you have bargained for. You may be a little vulnerable and you must pull back from this situation.

October 20th, Friday

You may find yourself in unfamiliar territory. Don't let this upset you or at least don't let it show if it does. You will now find that things in general may be a little hectic, but things will ease off and you will find out that you are on the right track.

October 21st, Saturday

You may need to pay a little more attention to yourself. You may have been neglecting yourself and it may be time to give yourself a treat, maybe a new image or some new clothes. You may find that you are attracting others and you will be in the spotlight for a little while.

October 22nd, Sunday

You may have cause for a small celebration today. You will enjoy family and friends' company today. It looks as if a family outing is on the cards. This will be an eye-opener, but don't let certain matters put you off as you will have not just a good day but also a very enjoyable evening.

October 23rd, Monday

A very unusual day lies ahead. Certain happenings may puzzle you, but try not to let your imagination run away with you. You will see things for what they really are and you'll be amazed with what has been going on right under your nose. However, you will find it quite amusing.

October 24th, Tuesday

At this time in your life you will benefit from plans that you have made in the past. Your personal life should now be on an upward turn. Money that changes hands will be very beneficial to you in the coming months and secure your future.

October 25th, Wednesday

You may get one-up on someone who has crossed you in the past. Try not to rub it in too much as what happens to them will not be pleasant. Your fate lies in your own hands today and you are finally in control of your life.

October 26th, Thursday

There will be certain changes with your work and these will be beneficial to you once the system is up and running. A stranger will give you good advice and point you in the right direction. If you have been worried about the romantic side of your life, this will be a time when things will all fall into place and the ball will be in your court.

October 27th, Friday

If you are planning to travel, this will be the perfect time to take a trip to the travel agent and make a booking. Try not to let them push you into a cheap deal as, if you take it, you will not be pleased with the outcome. Take time to think things through and you will not regret turning down a bargain.

October 28th, Saturday

You may have someone else's problems on your shoulders, but you must not take them too much to heart. You can make a great difference to someone's life just by giving them sound advice. This will ensure that you do not burden yourself with other people's stresses and worries.

October 29th, Sunday

Take time out for a loved one today as a partner may feel a little neglected. This will be a positive day with a positive outcome. A new chapter of your life is about to begin. It may turn out to be more than just a pleasant day.

October 30th, Monday

Take a good look around you and you'll be surprised at what you take for granted. You may feel a little stuck in a situation, but you'll soon move forward to better things. Try not to be impatient as you'll soon be moving into the fast lane.

October 31st, Tuesday

Someone may be eager to criticise you today, but let their words fly over your head. You must not play into their hands. Love matters may need some attention and you may find that you may have been missing out on certain matters.

NOVEMBER

November 1st, Wednesday

You'll be amazed at what takes place today. You will be over the moon with the news that you receive. A letter that you receive today may unsettle you, but this will be sorted out in a very short space of time. A loved one comes to your rescue and all will be well.

November 2nd, Thursday

You may have a deadline to meet. Try not to panic as you will get through all the work and meet it. Try not to be too hard on yourself as you really will deserve a pat on the back. You will deserve a treat, so pamper yourself and do something that you really enjoy doing.

November 3rd, Friday

A different light will be cast on a work situation and you'll be very surprised at what the outcome will be. To your surprise it will work out to your advantage. Don't worry about money matters as your purse will be full, but unfortunately not bottomless, so spend your cash with care.

November 4th, Saturday

Someone may try to take advantage of your good nature. Don't let them. You will see straight through them and can use the situation to obtain the information that you need. Let them down gently afterwards.

November 5th, Sunday

Look back into your past and try to remember the good times. This will put you in a good mood. You will certainly need to be at your best today in order to impress someone in power who could help you in the near future. Advancement is foreseen and you will be offered a better position or another way to earn your living.

November 6th, Monday

You may be missing out today if you don't keep your eyes open as something very good will come your way. Try not to let it pass you by. Someone may be trying to get your attention. It would be to your advantage if you show some interest as this will help you to advance.

November 7th, Tuesday

Today life will be full of fun and adventure. This will be the start of a completely new project in which you will want to be involved. Get ready to cover new ground and learn many new things. You will have your eyes opened today. Enjoy it while it lasts as you will not forget what you see today.

November 8th, Wednesday

You may be putting yourself down in many ways. Try to have more confidence. You need to have a more positive outlook as you are entering a new chapter in your life. This will open your eyes to the many opportunities that you could take.

November 9th, Thursday

What a day this will be. It will start off in rather an unusual way. Let your hair down as you'll need a rather carefree approach. Today will run very smoothly and you'll be in a good frame of mind. It will be a good day for dealing with people.

November 10th, Friday

This is a new day with a new direction and you will be more than pleased with what happens. You will find that a happy atmosphere surrounds you. There will be some good news, maybe something that you have been waiting for. Try not to get overexcited or you may wear yourself out.

November 11th, Saturday

If you find out a secret today, don't act on impulse as you may have got the wrong end of the stick. Find out all the facts before you take any action. The phone may ring and you may not be interested in the person at the other end. Grin and bear it as they may just have some news which will cast a new light on your situation.

November 12th, Sunday

You should be in a better frame of mind today. If you look back over the past week, you will find out that you have got a lot done and you will have less on your mind. Have a day out and relax.

November 13th, Monday

Love matters are set to improve and, if you are single, this will be a good time to meet that perfect love. Plan a night out on the town – it will work wonders.

November 14th, Tuesday

Planetary influences indicate that new acquaintances are about to enter your life. They will open many doors for you. New friends will be made, too, and with new friends comes new money. This will make your life less complicated and will ensure that you will have no more setbacks.

November 15th, Wednesday

You may be in two minds over what to do about love matters. You may feel like walking away from a current partner, but would you be doing the right thing? It would not be wise to act on impulse. Take a break and have a good think before you act. Your mind will then be clearer and you will know exactly what you must do.

November 16th, Thursday

You may feel unsettled in your work environment, but the situation will soon work out to your advantage. A letter that you receive today will simplify your problems and will only inspire you to work harder at getting things right.

November 17th, Friday

If you have a secret, now is the right time to share it. A loved one or close friend will be amused by your story and at the same time you will get things off your chest.

November 18th, Saturday

You may think that today will be no different from any other Saturday. To your surprise today will turn out to be very exciting and it will bring more than you ever expected. This will be the beginning of not only a new friendship but a whole new direction.

November 19th, Sunday

You will hear news that you will receive some money. Try not to spend it before you receive it as it may take a little longer to go into your bank account than you think. However, money will come eventually and you'll have less cause to worry.

November 20th, Monday

A family member will bring very good news and there may be plans to have a celebration. This may come at a very inconvenient time, but try to keep a little time aside to join in with the family fun. You won't regret it.

November 21st, Tuesday

Someone may be dragging you down with their depressing attitude. It will do you no good to hang out with such company as they will only bring you down to their level. Give your other friends a call and you'll soon be feeling more cheerful.

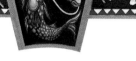

November 22nd, Wednesday

You may feel a little worried about a long-standing family problem, but all will be resolved and sooner than you think. You must try not to worry so much as this does not help your situation. You will be pleased to know that your luck will soon get better and money matters are set to improve.

November 23rd, Thursday

You may have been searching for something special and you may now feel like giving up. Don't give in just yet as you never know just what is around the corner. I can tell you that there are very good times ahead.

November 24th, Friday

You will have a change of mind about the direction in which your life is currently running. Try not to be too quick to change certain matters as your life is set to change for the better of its own accord.

November 25th, Saturday

Someone close to you may think that they have everything under control. You may be in just the right place at the right time and you will be able to step in and save the day. You will be widely praised for this and it will put you back in the limelight.

November 26th, Sunday

You can make a difference to your life if you put your mind to it, but you may need a little push now and again. It's high time that you started to push yourself forward a little of your own accord. After all, you do not really want someone else to take the credit.

November 27th, Monday

You may have to let something go and you may feel as if you are taking a step backwards. Really you are taking a step forwards. The loss will be a blessing in disguise and you will soon feel at home with the changes that you have just made.

November 28th, Tuesday

Someone may be on your mind. If you are worried, pick up the phone and give them a call. You will soon find that everything is all right. You are just a natural born worrier and you'll be surprised just how well things are going. At least this will put your mind at rest.

November 29th, Wednesday

You may be very tempted to do something very out of the ordinary, but are you sure that you are not getting yourself into a situation that will not get out of so easily? Have a good think about it and ask yourself if it is this really worth it. If it is, then go ahead.

November 30th, Thursday

You'll probably be very pleased that this month is nearly over as it has been a bit hectic. However, better times lie directly ahead and you will be all the wiser for what you have been through. Get ready for a good month as it will bring new opportunities and happiness into your life.

DECEMBER

December 1st, Friday

Your life should now be moving into the fast lane and you may find it may be going a little too fast for you. However, it will not stay in the fast lane and will soon slow to a more comfortable speed. You should expect to make new friends and move on to a higher plane.

December 2nd, Saturday

If you have been thinking of putting a keep-fit plan into action this would be the perfect time to do so. Try to spend a little more time with a loved one as they may be feeling a little low.

December 3rd, Sunday

Someone may drop a bombshell today and this may not please you. Try to look into it a little deeper as you may find that things are not really as bad as they seem. The problem that involves you will soon fade into the distance.

December 4th, Monday

A shopping spree may be on the cards today. Try not to buy too much as you may find you will go over your budget. You must cut down a little as you will need money for another time. Try to put a little to one side as you may need a little extra cash in the future.

December 5th, Tuesday

You may have Christmas on your mind. This may be a good time to think about it and make a start on the present list. This will save you time and money. If you start early, you will have no cause to panic later on.

December 6th, Wednesday

You may be told a secret from which you will benefit greatly. This will put you on guard in a future situation. When someone tells you or hints about what you have been told, on no account reveal that you already know.

December 7th, Thursday

You may be invited to a party. Make sure that your partner is happy with the situation before you accept. Someone from the past may get in touch with you.

December 8th, Friday

You may be looking at your life too closely. Try not to be dissatisfied with your lot. Soon you will change the direction that you are in. You will benefit from a friendship and a friend will bring something good into your life.

December 9th, Saturday

You will now be on the right track and going in the right direction. Don't be too eager to get into a new business venture as planetary influences indicate that a bigger and better opportunity lies at your feet and will soon be revealed to you.

December 10th, Sunday

You may receive an offer from someone that seems very hard to refuse. This may be a good opportunity, but try to look at it very closely as there may be a catch to it. Be on your guard and ask plenty of questions. You may see this person for what they really are.

December 11th, Monday

Good connections will be made today and after what takes place you will never look back. You have now entered a new chapter of your life and your life will take a turn for the better. Money matters will be moving forward fast.

December 12th, Tuesday

Don't let others make your life a misery. Stand your ground and don't let anyone push you around. You may need to speak your mind and let people know just where they stand. This will ensure that you will not be taken advantage of again.

December 13th, Wednesday

A letter that you receive today will certainly brighten your day. There will be plans made for the future and these plans that you make now will certainly come off. You will benefit by a loved one's suggestions.

December 14th, Thursday

Someone who has done you wrong in the past will try to get around you. However, there may be some method in their madness. Try not to do them any favours as they will not be returned. Don't let your heart rule your head as you may be in for a bit if a difficult day. You will hear some good news which will make a satisfying end to your working day.

December 15th, Friday

If a bill lands on your doorstep today, try not to panic as it will not be as large as you imagined. If you are thinking of making major changes, now is the perfect time to do so. A loved one will try to spoil your good mood. Try not to play into their hands and leave them to themselves.

December 16th, Saturday

You may be feeling irritable today and people may be getting on your nerves. You may have a lot to do. You'll get through it all, but not without a little aggravation from a family member. Try not to be side-tracked and you'll get things done.

December 17th, Sunday

If you are a feeling little tired, make sure that you have a good rest as you have an exciting but hectic week ahead. You may get a visit from a family member and with it will come some gossip. Let it go in one ear and out of the other, as probably none of it will be true. Ignore it, but try to look interested. Love matters will improve today and you are in for quite a treat tonight.

December 18th, Monday

If you are about to go shopping, then you are in for a treat as there will be plenty of bargains to be had. Try not to buy anything that you don't really have much use for as you will eventually find that special something that you have had your eye on for some time. Save the best for last and save your cash. Planetary influences indicate that your love life will get a real boost today.

December 19th, Tuesday

Listen to your heart when you are faced with a decision. New business plans will crop up out of the blue and what happens today will govern your future. Major changes are about to take place and your life will improve immensely.

December 20th, Wednesday

What you hear on the grapevine will benefit you greatly if you act now. Someone may try to put you off acting, but take no notice as they have their own reasons. Keep your ideas to yourself as someone may use your ideas and benefit before you do. Secrecy is the key if you wish to advance.

December 21st, Thursday

You may accidentally find out something that you have wanted to know. Some idle gossip will give you the

information that you have needed for some time now. Use this information to your own advantage, but try not to tell anyone else as they may try to steal your ideas. Keep your success to yourself for a little while.

December 22nd, Friday

You may find that you are faced with a rather exciting challenge today. What you originally thought impossible will be within your reach. However, you will be very pleased with the outcome of today's events. Many new doors will open and problems that you have encountered will be solved.

December 23rd, Saturday

You may have some last-minute shopping to do. Family and friends may be making demands on you. Try to organise the day and all will be well. This evening promises to be full of fun and laughter.

December 24th, Sunday

It's Christmas Eve and what a day this will be. You may have forgotten a special present for someone. Go through your list and you may realise that you have forgotten someone. This evening will be one to remember and what takes place today will change your life.

December 25th, Monday

Happy Christmas! You will be surrounded by a lot of presents today. You may receive a surprise. You will be very pleased with what takes place today. Try to relax a little as the fun will really take off today and there will be a lot of enjoyment. Planetary influences indicate that love matters will please you in many ways. This will be the perfect time to draw closer to a loved one.

December 26th, Tuesday

Planetary influences indicate that you will receive very good news today. Money matters are set to improve and you will make changes for the better on the home front.

December 27th, Wednesday

You may need to put your feet up for a while as you may have been burning the candle at both ends. Love will bring changes for the better and a pleasant surprise is just around the corner.

December 28th, Thursday

If a loved one tries to advise you into parting with cash, try to stick to your own opinion as you will regret parting with your money today. Keep away from the shops and you will be away from temptation.

December 29th, Friday

You may be feeling a little restless today. As the end of the year draws closer you may wonder what the coming year will bring. However, you will be surprised at how well it will go. You may find that you are worrying over small matters.

December 30th, Saturday

Plans that you have made in the past will fall into place today. A major change is foreseen and this will be for the better. Improvements to your life will happen sooner than you think.

December 31st, Sunday

This will be a day to remember. When the bells ring out at midnight you will feel relieved that the year has finally come to an end.

The coming year will be one to remember. Planetary influences indicate that you will have changes for the better with money matters and your love life will improve tremendously.

Wishing you seven years' kusty bok (good luck).
All the best for the coming year, and may all
your dreams come true.

James Petulengro